JUL   2009

W9-CJD-133

MAP TYPES

ALL OVER THE MAP

Ann Becker

Crabtree Publishing Company

www.crabtreebooks.com

Crabtree Publishing Company

www.crabtreebooks.com

Author: Ann Becker
Coordinating editor: Chester Fisher
Series editor: Scholastic Ventures
Project editor: Robert Walker
Editor: Reagan Miller
Proofreaders: Molly Aloian, Crystal Sikkens
Production coordinator: Katherine Kantor
Prepress technicians: Katherine Kantor, Ken Wright
Project manager: Santosh Vasudevan (Q2AMEDIA)
Art direction: Rahul Dhiman (Q2AMEDIA)
Cover design: Nikhil Bhutani (Q2AMEDIA)
Design: Dibakar Acharjee (Q2AMEDIA)
Photo research: Anju Pathak (Q2AMEDIA)

Photographs:
123RF: Olya Tropinina: p. 27
Aerialarchives: p. 18, 21
Alamy: Jim Havey: p. 6
BigStockPhoto: EventureMan: p. 16; IndianSummer: p. 11
Buckminster Fuller Institute: p. 29
City and County of Denver and Downtown Denver Partnership: p. 7
Digital Data Services: p. 1, 17
Drozdp: p. 12
Istockphoto: Mike Bentley: cover (bottom left); Jami Garrison: p. 9;
    Natasha Japp: p. 31
Mapsofworld.com: p. 30
Nationalatlas.gov: p. 5, 10, 15 (top), 23
National Oceanic and Atmospheric Administration: p. 4, 24, 25
Photolibrary: cover (top left)
Radar.weather.gov: p. 22
Shutterstock: Jamie Cross: p. 13; Inger Anne Hulbækdal: p. 8;
    Kerrie Jones: p. 14–15; Gabriel Moisa: cover (background);
    Pakhnyushcha: p. 26; Taipan Kid: p. 28
TerraServer: p. 20
Usgs.gov: p. 19

Illustrations:
Q2AMedia

Library and Archives Canada Cataloguing in Publication

Becker, Ann, 1965-
    Map types / Ann Becker.

(All over the map)
Includes index.
ISBN 978-0-7787-4269-2 (bound).--ISBN 978-0-7787-4274-6 (pbk.)

    1. Maps--Juvenile literature. I. Title. II. Series: All over the map
(St. Catharines, Ont.)

GA105.6.S25 2008   j912   C2008-903496-1

Library of Congress Cataloging-in-Publication Data

Becker, Ann, 1965-
  Map types / Ann Becker.
      p. cm. -- (All over the map)
  Includes index.
  ISBN-13: 978-0-7787-4274-6 (pbk. : alk. paper)
  ISBN-10: 0-7787-4274-1 (pbk. : alk. paper)
  ISBN-13: 978-0-7787-4269-2 (reinforced library binding : alk. paper)
  ISBN-10: 0-7787-4269-5 (reinforced library binding : alk. paper)
  1. Maps--Juvenile literature. I. Title. II. Series.

  GA105.6.B43 2009
  912--dc22
                                                    2008023528

Crabtree Publishing Company

www.crabtreebooks.com   1-800-387-7650

Published in Canada
Crabtree Publishing
616 Welland Ave.
St. Catharines, Ontario
L2M 5V6

Published in the United States
Crabtree Publishing
PMB16A
350 Fifth Ave., Suite 3308
New York, NY 10118

Published in the United Kingdom
Crabtree Publishing
White Cross Mills
High Town, Lancaster
LA1 4XS

Published in Australia
Crabtree Publishing
386 Mt. Alexander Rd.
Ascot Vale (Melbourne)
VIC 3032

CONTENTS

What is a Map?   4

Street Maps   6

Atlases   8

Political Maps   10

More About Political Maps   12

Physical Maps   14

More Physical Maps   16

Topographic Maps   18

More Topographic Maps   20

Weather Maps   22

Bigger Weather Maps   24

Globes   26

Globes and Flat Maps   28

Specialty Maps   30

Glossary and Index   32

What is a Map?

Maps are drawings of a place. But the drawings are not art. They give people **information**, or facts, about the place.

There are different kinds of maps. Each kind of map shows different information. For example, the weather map below tells people what the weather will be like in different places.

———————————— WEATHER MAP ————————————

Snow

A.M. Snow

Heavy Snow Likely

Rain

Snow

P.M. Snow

Rain

P.M. Rain

Heavy Snow Possible

Flooding Possible

A.M. Rain

Rain/ T'Storms

Severe T'Storms Possible

Rain/ T'Storms

A.M. Rain

This map shows the weather.

4

The map on this page shows the United States, too. But it gives different information. It gives the names of all of the states. So maps can show the same place, but give different information.

Let's keep reading to learn what these maps, and more, can teach you!

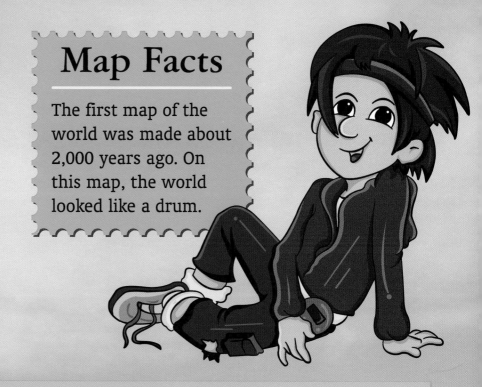

Map Facts

The first map of the world was made about 2,000 years ago. On this map, the world looked like a drum.

------------- MAP OF THE UNITED STATES -------------

▲ *This map names the states.*

Street Maps

The map and photo show the same place in different ways.

This picture shows the streets in Denver.

Street maps show the streets in a town or city. I see that both the picture and the map show streets in Denver. The picture and the map are of the same part of town. The picture tells me what the streets look like. The map shows me a whole lot more.

This is a Denver street map. If I needed to go somewhere, I could use the map to find my way.

The map shows the names of the streets. Street maps have a **compass rose** that shows which way is north, south, east, or west. When I read a map to find a street, I look for which way the street goes. Then I look for what streets are nearby. I use this information to find my way.

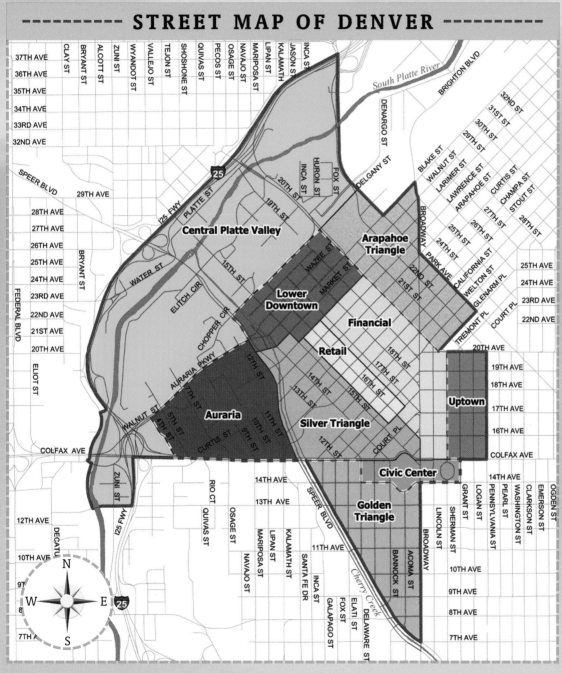

This map shows the streets in Denver.

Atlases

On long trips, drivers use large road maps, or **atlases**.
Atlases show larger areas than street maps. Instead
of streets in a city, an atlas can show a whole state.
A driver uses an atlas to plan what roads to drive on.

▲ *Drivers use atlases to plan long trips.*

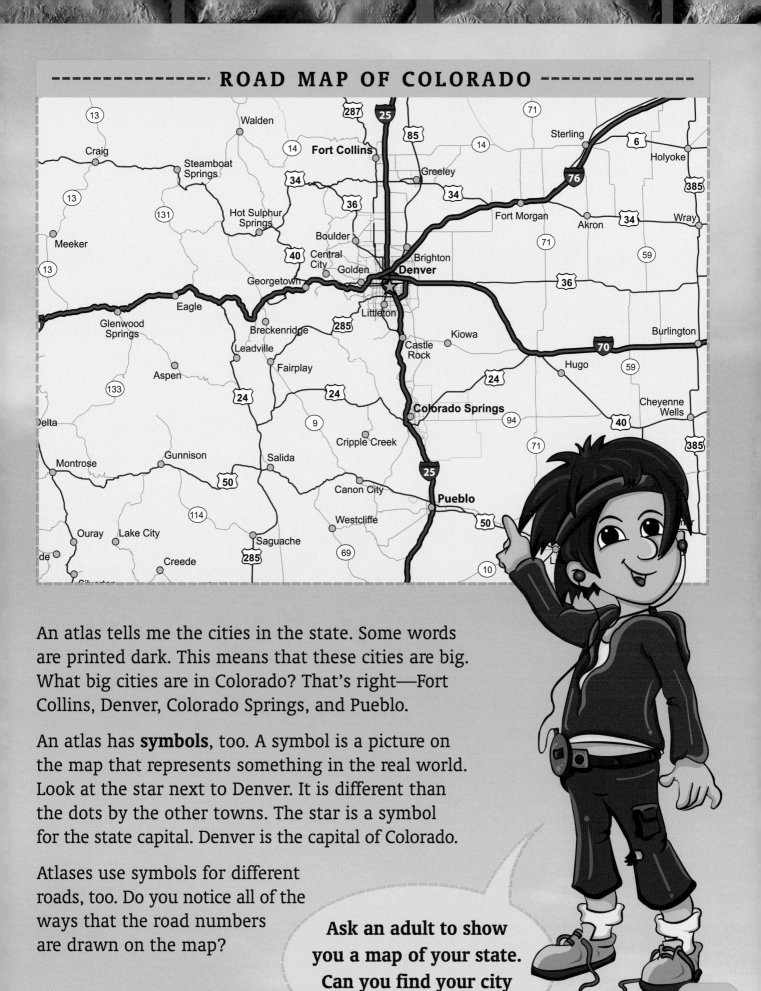

An atlas tells me the cities in the state. Some words are printed dark. This means that these cities are big. What big cities are in Colorado? That's right—Fort Collins, Denver, Colorado Springs, and Pueblo.

An atlas has **symbols**, too. A symbol is a picture on the map that represents something in the real world. Look at the star next to Denver. It is different than the dots by the other towns. The star is a symbol for the state capital. Denver is the capital of Colorado.

Atlases use symbols for different roads, too. Do you notice all of the ways that the road numbers are drawn on the map?

Ask an adult to show you a map of your state. Can you find your city on the map?

9

Political Maps

Some maps tell about government. They are called **political maps**. Political maps show lines that separate places, such as countries, states, or counties. Political maps show rivers, lakes, and oceans, too. This map shows the countries in North America. It has lines between the countries. It also shows the oceans, large rivers, and lakes. So it is a political map of North America.

Map Facts

Any political map can be colored using only four colors. The trick is that no touching sections can be the same color.

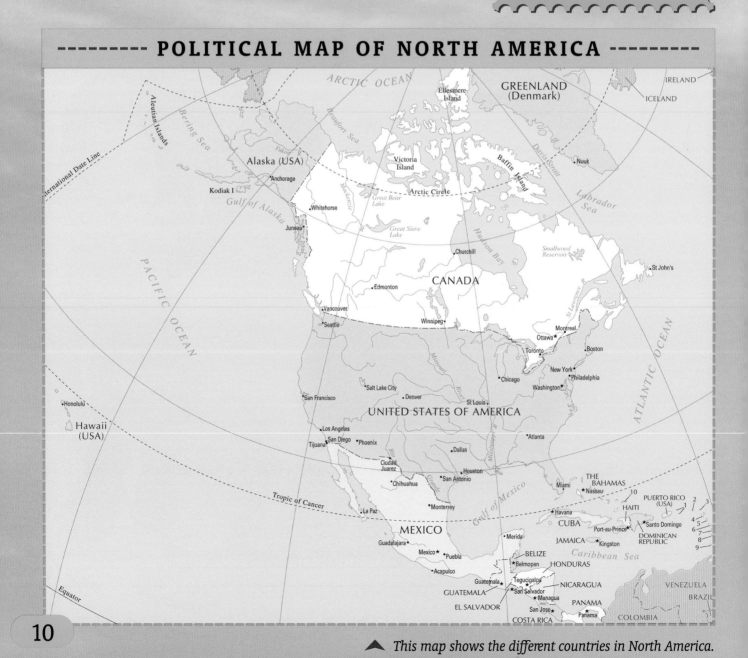

-------- **POLITICAL MAP OF NORTH AMERICA** ---------

This map shows the different countries in North America.

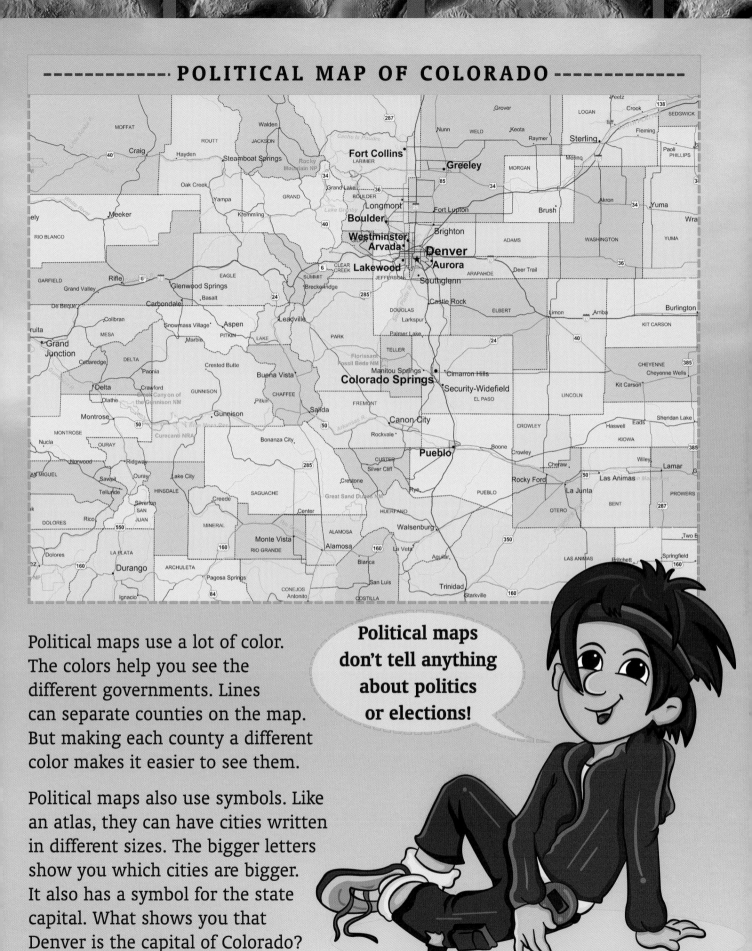

Political maps use a lot of color. The colors help you see the different governments. Lines can separate counties on the map. But making each county a different color makes it easier to see them.

Political maps also use symbols. Like an atlas, they can have cities written in different sizes. The bigger letters show you which cities are bigger. It also has a symbol for the state capital. What shows you that Denver is the capital of Colorado?

Political maps don't tell anything about politics or elections!

More About Political Maps

The map on page 11 was a political map of one state. Political maps can show larger pieces of land, too!

A **border** is a line that divides two different parts of land. In the political map of Colorado, there are borders around each county. In a political map of a country, there are borders around each state.

These lines are not part of the land. Look at the picture of the Four Corners. This is the spot where Colorado, New Mexico, Utah, and Arizona meet. The marker shows where the four corners of the states meet. But there is no line on the ground separating the states.

There are political maps of whole continents. Each country is a different color. You can see the borders between the countries, too.

Some political maps show bodies of water, such as oceans, large lakes, and rivers. The water might be on the border of a state or country.

▲ *This monument is on the ground where the borders of four states meet. It is called "The Four Corners."*

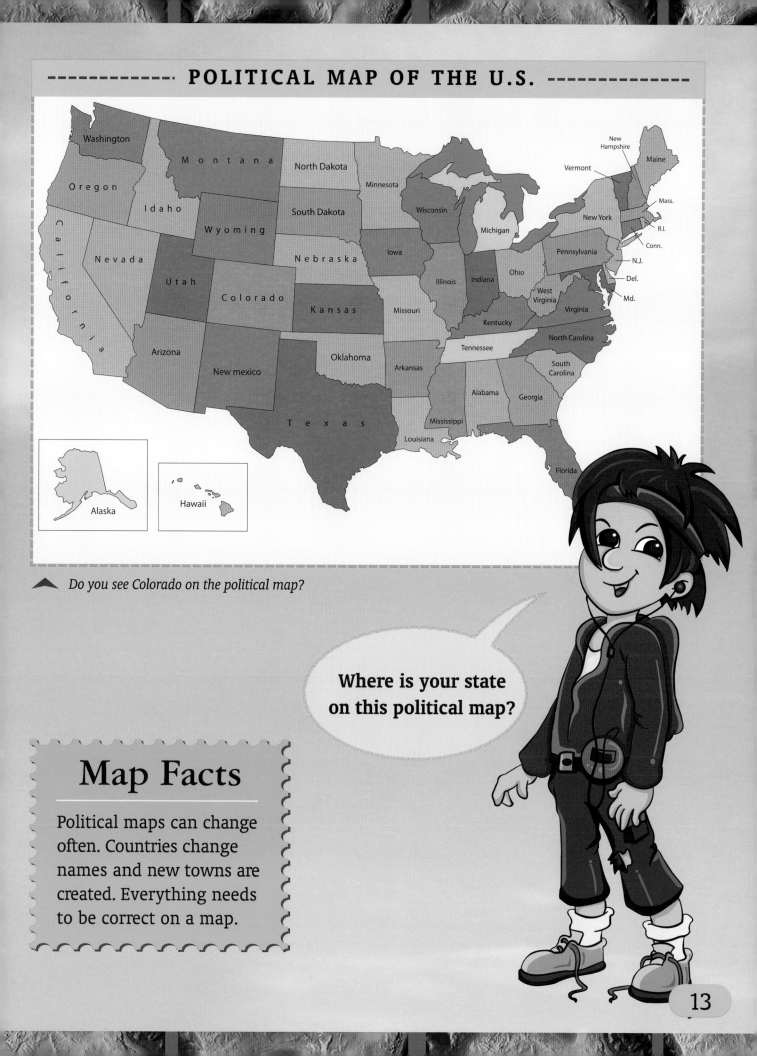

Do you see Colorado on the political map?

Where is your state on this political map?

Map Facts

Political maps can change often. Countries change names and new towns are created. Everything needs to be correct on a map.

Physical Maps

How do I know where oceans, lakes, and rivers are? What about mountains? Road maps and political maps don't tell me this. But **physical maps** do. A physical map shows bodies of water and **landforms**, such as mountains or valleys.

This is a physical map of Colorado. I don't see any oceans, and very few lakes. I can see rivers, though. They are thin, blue lines.

A physical map shows different landforms, too. Look at the picture. It shows the Rocky Mountains. Now look at the map. The Rocky Mountains are in the center of the state. The label makes them easy to find.

▼ *The Rocky Mountains are beautiful! They run right through Colorado.*

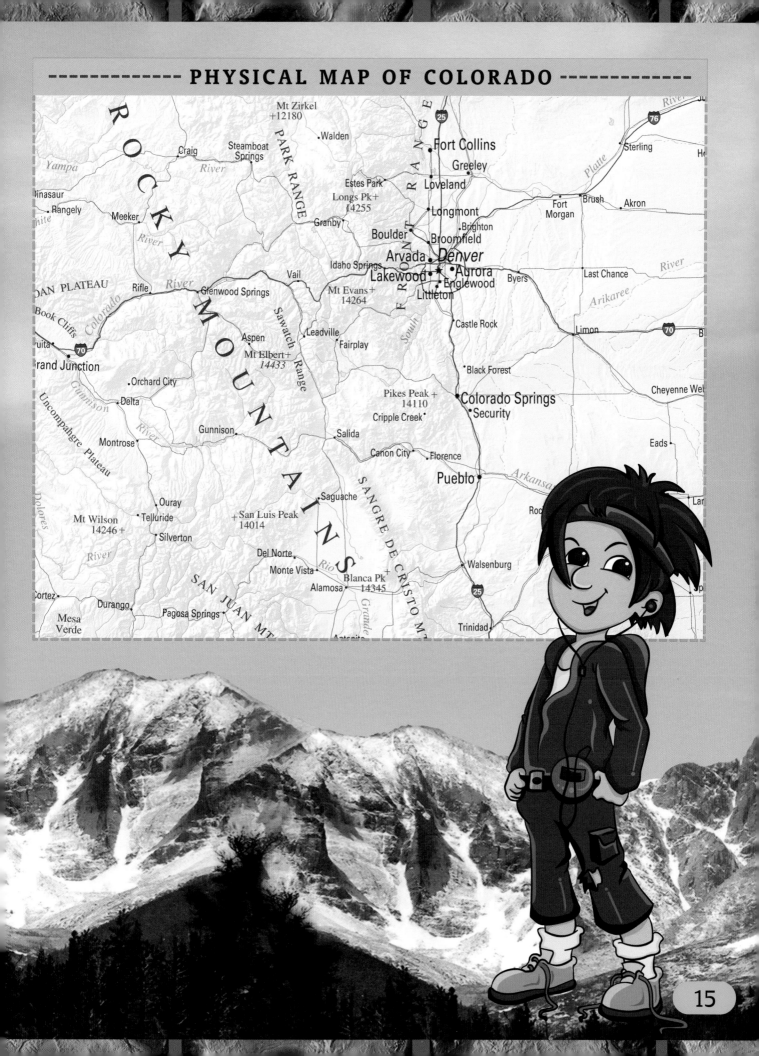

PHYSICAL MAP OF COLORADO

Mt Zirkel +12180

Walden

ROCKY

Yampa

River

Craig

Steamboat Springs

PARK RANGE

Dinosaur

Rangely

Estes Park

Longs Pk +14255

Granby

FRONT RANGE

Fort Collins

Greeley

Loveland

Longmont

Brighton

Fort Morgan

Brush

Sterling

He

Akron

Meeker

River

Boulder

Broomfield

Denver

Platte

River

N PLATEAU

Rifle

River

Glenwood Springs

Vail

Idaho Springs

Arvada

Lakewood

Aurora

Englewood

Byers

Last Chance

Arikaree

River

Book Cliffs

Colorado

uita

Grand Junction

70

Sawatch Range

Mt Evans +14264

Leadville

Littleton

Castle Rock

Limon

70

B

Aspen

Mt Elbert +14433

Fairplay

South

Black Forest

Cheyenne Wel

Orchard City

Gunnison

Delta

River

Gunnison

Pikes Peak +14110

Colorado Springs

Security

Montrose

Salida

Cripple Creek

Eads

Uncompahgre Plateau

Saguache

Canon City

Florence

Arkansas

Lar

Ouray

Tellluride

San Luis Peak 14014

Pueblo

Roc

Dolores

Mt Wilson 14246 +

Silverton

SANGRE DE CRISTO MT

Cortez

Del Norte

Monte Vista

Rio

Blanca Pk 14345

Alamosa

Walsenburg

River

Durango

Pagosa Springs

SAN JUAN MT

Grande

25

Mesa Verde

Antonito

Trinidad

15

More Physical Maps

Physical maps show landforms. Adding details to the maps can show the shape of the land. Colors help you tell these landforms apart, too. How do **cartographers**, or map makers, use color to show different kinds of land?

In the Denver map and photograph, I see mountains and plains. The plains are hard to see on a large map. But when you make a map of a smaller place, the landforms are more noticeable.

▲ *The land changes a lot as you travel through Denver!*

Craig
Steamboat
Springs
Fort Collins
Sterling
Estes Park
25
Greeley
Longmont
76
Fort Morgan
Boulder
Golden
DENVER
70
Vail
70
Castle Rock
Rifle
Glenwood
Springs
70
Aspen
25
Grand Junction
Colorado Springs
Montrose
Gunnison
Salida
Pueblo
La Junta
25
Alamosa
ez
Durango
Trinidad

▲ *Find landmarks on the map, such as the mountains, roads, and plains.*

Cartographers sometimes put rivers and mountains on maps. This is because they are **landmarks**. Landmarks are things that you can see, and they do not move. Physical maps include landmarks. Landmarks help you find your way. If a school is next to a lake, the lake is a landmark that makes the school easier to find.

Topographic Maps

This is a really useful map! It is called a **topographic map**. A topographic map uses lines to show the shape of the land. At first, that sounds a lot like a physical map. But topographic maps look at smaller pieces of land, and use lines in different ways than physical maps.

This map and picture show the same place. But look at the picture. Everything looks flat. That's where the topographic map helps. All those curvy lines, called **contour lines**, show where the land changes shape.

Put your finger on one line and follow it. Everywhere you touch on the map would be the same level on land. In other words, if you walked exactly where the line is, you would never go up or down. It would be flat.

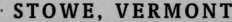

STOWE, VERMONT

▲ *The picture makes the land look flat.*

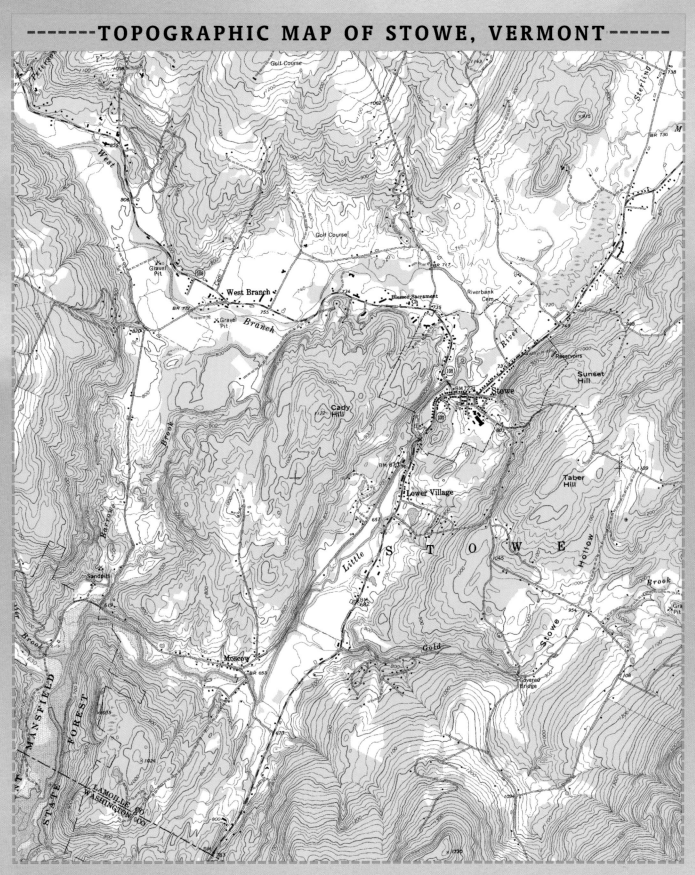

The picture and map both show Stowe, Vermont. But the map has contour lines. The lines show how the land changes shape.

More Topographic Maps

I remember contour lines show the land changing shape. I also know that if I follow one line, I travel in a flat path. So how does the map show hills?

The map shows hills when you move from one line to the next. Imagine stepping from one line to another. You either step up or down. How do you know which? Every line has a number. The number is the **elevation**. Elevation is how high above the sea any place is. If the number goes up from one line to the next, you go up a hill. If the number goes down, you step down.

It is hard to see hills in this picture!

-------------------- PHOTO OF CHERRY CREEK --------------------

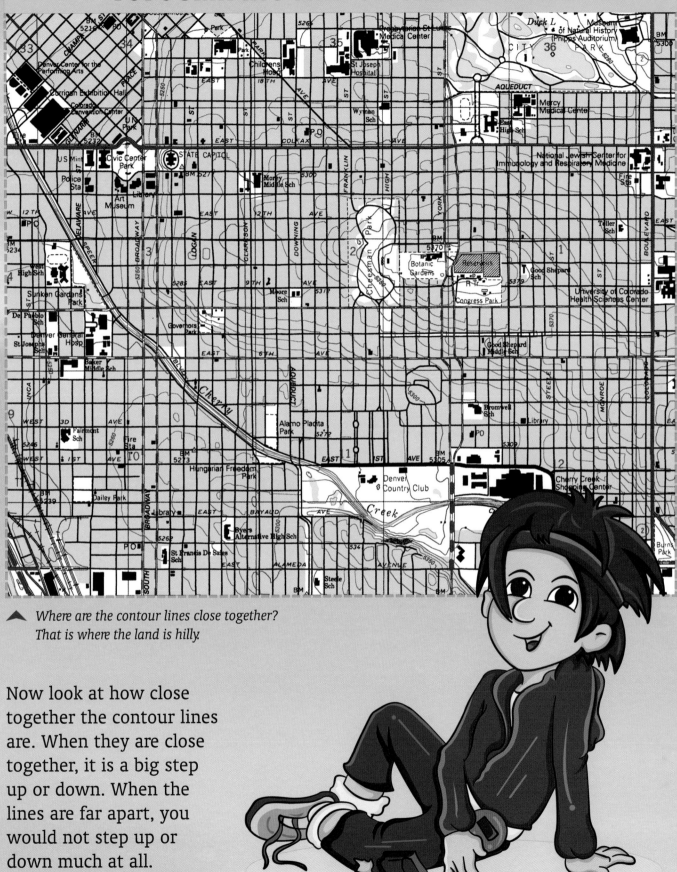

TOPOGRAPHIC MAP OF CHERRY CREEK

▲ *Where are the contour lines close together?*
That is where the land is hilly.

Now look at how close together the contour lines are. When they are close together, it is a big step up or down. When the lines are far apart, you would not step up or down much at all.

Weather Maps

You may have never seen a topographic map. But I bet you have seen this! Weather maps show people what the weather is like. If I look at a weather map, I can make sure I dress for rain, snow, or a hot, sunny day. I can also plan. I wouldn't plan a picnic with my mom if I knew it was going to rain.

▼ *You can see weather maps in the news every day!*

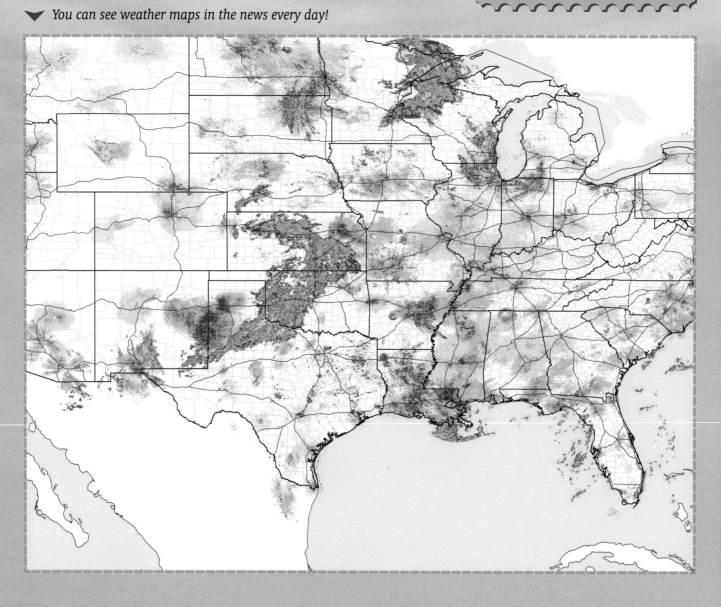

Snake River

Little

N. Platte River

Cache la Poudre R.

River

Yampa

River

Platte

White

Lake Granby

Box Elder Cr.

Beaver Creek

River

Colorado River

Blue R.

River

Arikaree

S Fk Republican

Gunnison River

South

Cherry Creek

Dolores

Blue Mesa Res

San Miguel

Uncompahgre R.

River

R.

Arkansas

McPhee Res

R.

Animas

Rio

Huerfano

R.

River

Apishapa

Purgatoire River

Mancos

Grande

Navajo

▲ On a weather map, you can see which areas will receive rain by looking at the area covered by the green patch.

Look at the green color on the map. People who live in these areas should prepare for bad weather. People should carry umbrellas if they are outside.

The green sections on the map look like clouds. But because this is a weather map, it shows rain. Different colors on the map can show mist, snow, or rain. Colors can also show different temperatures.

Bigger Weather Maps

This is a picture from space. It shows what the weather is like for many states. I know it is a map because I see state borders. Those lines are not on the land. They are drawn in.

---------------------- WEATHER MAP OF U.S. ----------------------

▲ *This map is a combination of pictures and drawings. The borders are drawn. The land, water, and clouds are in the photograph.*

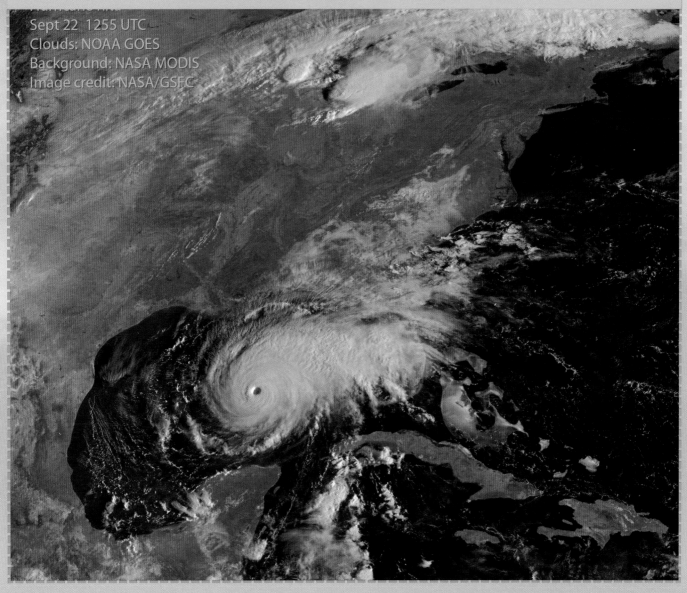

Sept 22 1255 UTC
Clouds: NOAA GOES
Background: NASA MODIS
Image credit: NASA/GSFC

▲ *This picture was taken from space. You can see a hurricane, named Rita, moving into the Gulf of Mexico.*

The clouds in the picture are not drawn in the weather map. Instead, the map shows the weather with photographs. For example, at the bottom of the picture, you can see a **hurricane**, or a huge storm, that moves in a circle.

But not every part of the country will have the hurricane. On the right side of the picture, there are very few clouds. People will enjoy nice weather in this area.

Map Facts

A person who studies the weather is a **meteorologist**.

Globes

A **globe** is a map that is in the shape of a ball. A globe might be a physical map, showing what the land looks like. Globes could be political maps, with borders of countries around the world. Globes could be both.

Globes are the closest map we have to the way Earth really looks. The planet is round, so the round map is a really good **model** of Earth. A model is a small copy of something else.

> I see names of places and borders on the globe. It is a political map.

What kind of map does this globe show?

Globes also show where all of the countries in the world are. If you put your finger on the United States, you can turn the globe to the opposite side and see what country is there. Could you do that on a flat map? Nope!

Which continent is on the opposite side of the globe from the United States?

Globes and Flat Maps

Globes do not fold up or store very well. That's why we make maps.

The problem with maps is that they are never as good a model as a globe. The map below is a rectangle. But Earth is round. If you covered the globe with this map, it wouldn't fit. This map is not the same shape as a globe, so parts of the world were stretched to make the rectangle. The shape and size of some countries or oceans will be a little "off."

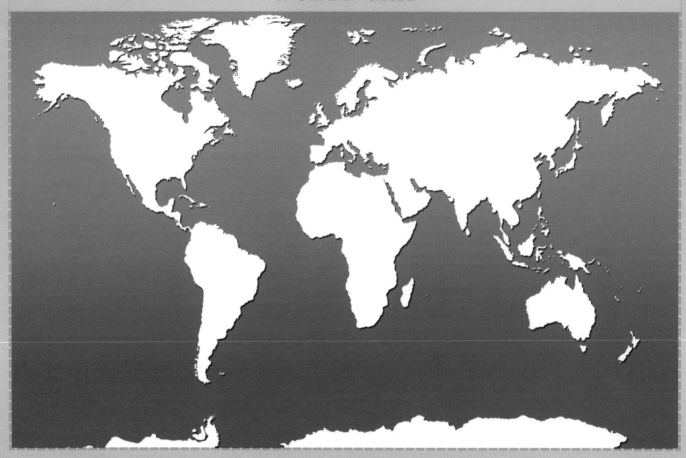

▲ *This map is shaped like a rectangle, even though the world is not. Places are stretched to fill the rectangle in.*

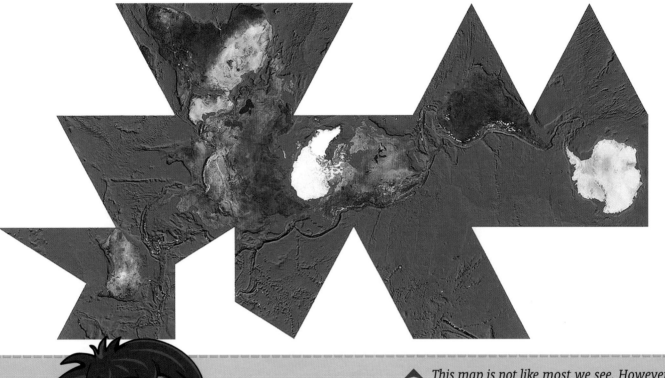

▲ *This map is not like most we see. However, no places are stretched to fill spaces.*

The map above looks like someone cut the globe apart, like peeling an orange. But now, the countries are not in the positions we are used to. There are also big gaps where the oceans should be connected. But at least the sizes are more correct than the map on page 28.

Map Facts

Rectangular maps can make some countries look larger or smaller than they really are.

Specialty Maps

We haven't talked about all the types of maps. There are more maps than we could ever talk about in one book.

Some jobs need special maps. A person putting in television cable wires needs maps to show where it is safe to dig. A person that takes care of computers in an office building could use a map to show where all of the computers are.

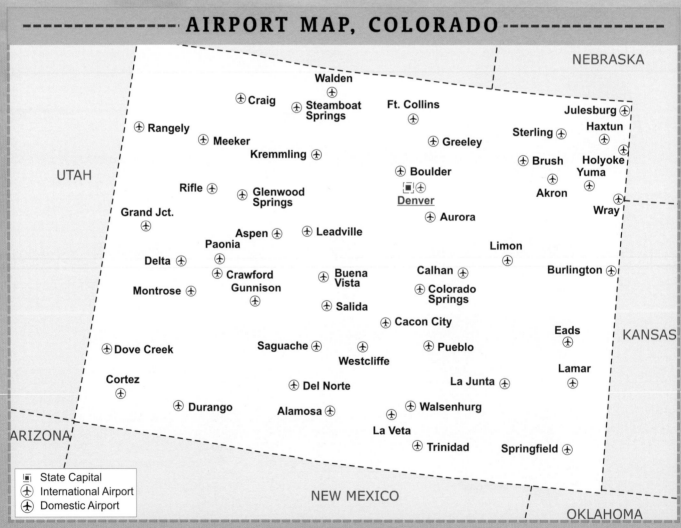

-------- AIRPORT MAP, COLORADO --------

NEBRASKA

Walden

Craig
Steamboat Springs
Ft. Collins
Julesburg
Haxtun

Rangely
Greeley
Sterling
Holyoke

UTAH
Meeker
Kremmling
Brush
Yuma

Boulder
Akron

Rifle
Glenwood Springs
Denver
Wray

Grand Jct.
Aurora

Aspen
Leadville
Limon

Paonia
Delta
Burlington

Crawford
Buena Vista
Calhan

Montrose
Gunnison
Colorado Springs

Salida

Cacon City
Eads
KANSAS

Dove Creek
Saguache
Pueblo

Westcliffe
Lamar

Cortez
Del Norte
La Junta

ARIZONA
Durango
Alamosa
Walsenhurg

La Veta

Trinidad
Springfield

Legend:
- ▣ State Capital
- ✈ International Airport
- ✈ Domestic Airport

NEW MEXICO

OKLAHOMA

▲ *Look how many airports Colorado has! This map would be helpful to a pilot.*

Hikers need special maps. A trail map shows where it is safe to hike. It also gives landmarks so hikers do not get lost.

Someone moving into a new neighborhood would love a map showing all the nearby businesses. Students going to a new school could use a school map to find their way around.

Maps help people find out where they are and where they need to go. Now I need to go!

Glossary

Note: Some boldfaced words are defined where they appear in the book.

atlas A map of roads in a state or country

border A line that divides two different parts of land

compass rose A drawing that shows north, south, east, and west

contour lines Lines that show changes of elevation

elevation How far above sea level a place is

landform A feature, such as a mountain, on Earth's surface

landmark Something you can see that does not move

meteorologist A person who studies the weather

physical map A map that shows bodies of water and landforms

political map A map that shows where governments are

symbol A shape or color that represents a building, place, or other part on a map

topographic map A map that shows changes in elevation

Index

atlas 8–9, 11

border 12, 24, 26

compass rose 7

continent 12, 27

contour lines 18, 19, 20, 21

elevation 20

globe 26, 27, 28, 29

government 10, 11

hurricane 25

label 14

landform 14, 16

landmark 17, 31

meteorologist 25

North America 10

physical map 14–17, 18, 26

political map 10–12, 13, 14, 26

Rocky Mountains 14, 15

streets/roads 6–7, 8, 9, 14, 17

symbol 9, 11

topographic map 18–21, 22

weather map 4, 22–25

Printed in the U.S.A. - CG